Ladybugs

and Other Beetles

Concept and Product Development: Editorial Options, Inc.
Series Designer: Karen Donica
Book Author: Steven Otfinoski

For information about other World Book publications, visit our
Web site at **http://www.worldbookonline.com** or call **1-800-WORLDBK (967-5325)**.
For information about sales to schools and libraries, call **1-800-975-3250**
(United States); 1-800-837-5365 (Canada).

2005 Revised printing

World Book, Inc.
233 N. Michigan Avenue
Chicago, IL 60601
U.S.A.

The Library of Congress has cataloged an earlier edition of this title as follows:

Otfinoski, Steven.
  Ladybugs and other beetles / [book author, Steven Otfinoski].
    p. cm. -- (World Book's animals of the world)
  Summary: Questions and answers explore the world of beetles,
with an emphasis on ladybugs.
  ISBN: 0-7166-1207-0
  1. Ladybugs--Juvenile literature. 2. Beetles--Juvenile literature.
  [I. Ladybugs--Miscellanea. 2. Beetles--Miscellanea. 3. Questions and answers.]
  I. World Book, Inc. II. Title. III. Series.
  QL596.C65 O83 2000
  595.76--dc21   00-021637

This edition:
Ladybugs: ISBN: 978-0-7166-1280-3
Set 1: ISBN: 978-0-7166-1273-5

Printed in China

6 7 8 9 10 12 11 10 09 08

Picture Acknowledgments: Cover: © Larry West, Bruce Coleman Inc.; © Jane Burton, Bruce Coleman Inc.; © Thomas Eisner & Daniel Aneshansley, Cornell University; © Ivan Polunin, Bruce Coleman Inc.; © Harry Rogers/NAS from Photo Researchers.

© Jane Burton, Bruce Coleman Inc. 37, 47; © Ken Brate, Photo Researchers 31; © Arlyn Evans, AG Stock USA 21; © Gregory Dimijian, Photo Researchers 9, 39; © Robert Dunne, Photo Researchers 53; © Robert L. Dunne, Bruce Coleman Inc. 27; © Thomas Eisner & Daniel Aneshansley, Cornell University, 33; © Dan Guravich, Photo Researchers 9; © David Hosking, Photo Researchers 9; © Jacques Jangoux, Photo Researchers 57; © Stephen Dalton, Photo Researchers 13; © Mark Moffett, Minden Pictures 35, 59, 61; © Stephen P. Parker, Photo Researchers 55; © Rod Planck, Photo Researchers 9 ; © Ivan Polunin, Bruce Coleman Inc. 25, 29; © David T. Roberts/Nature's Images Inc. from Photo Researchers 19; © Harry Rogers/NAS, from Photo Researchers 15, 23; © Edward S. Ross, 43, 51; © Gregory K. Scott, Photo Researchers 49; © Waina Cheng Ward, Bruce Coleman Collection 11; © Larry West, Bruce Coleman Inc. 7; © Konrad Wothe, Minden Pictures 17; © Bruce Davidson, Animals Animals 45

Illustrations: WORLD BOOK illustration by Michael DiGiorgio 41; WORLD BOOK illustration by Patricia Stein 62.

World Book's Animals of the World

Ladybugs
and Other Beetles

WORLD
BOOK

a Scott Fetzer company
Chicago
www.worldbookonline.com

Contents

What makes me click?

How do I beat the heat?

Why do we have a special glow?

What Is a Beetle?

Beetles are one group of insects. There are at least 300,000 kinds, or species, of beetles. That is more kinds than any other animal on the earth. About 40 percent of all insects are beetles.

Beetles come in many shapes and sizes. The feather-winged beetle is less than 1/50 of an inch (0.5 millimeter) long. The Goliath *(guh LY uhth)* beetle grows up to 5 inches (13 centimeters). Some beetles have big snouts. Others have long antennae *(an TEHN ee).* Some have jaws that look like antlers.

Beetles come in many different colors. Some beetles are black or dull brown. Others are bright green, gold, or red. Some, like the ladybug you see here, have spots. Others have stripes.

Ladybug

Where in the World Do Beetles Live?

Beetles live nearly everywhere on the earth. The only places they don't live are the oceans.

Beetles can be found in deserts, rain forests, grasslands, and freezing cold places. Beetles live on mountains, in lakes and streams, on plains, and in meadows. Beetles have adapted their bodies and their behavior to different climates and conditions. Beetles are great survivors. They were on the earth long before people were.

Desert

Rain forest

Grassland

Ice region

How Many Spots Does a Ladybug Have?

It varies. Most ladybugs share certain features. They have small, pea-shaped bodies and six short legs. Most ladybugs are less than 1/4 inch (6.35 millimeters) long. But ladybugs differ in their spots!

Most ladybugs have spots on their backs. The spots may be black, red, white, or yellow. Some kinds of ladybugs have 13 spots. Others have only 2 spots. The color of the body may be black, bright red, orange, or yellow.

Often you can see a ladybug's bright back and spots from a distance. There is a good reason for this. Ladybugs taste bitter, and their color pattern is a warning to hungry birds and other animals to stay away. It reminds enemies that ladybugs are not good to eat.

Ladybugs with different patterns

How Are Ladybugs Like Armored Tanks?

The ladybug has a special pair of wings that protect its body from enemies. These tough, leatherlike wings are called elytra *(EHL uh truh)*. The elytra are attached to the front of the ladybug and cover the set of wings underneath. Most beetles have elytra.

When the ladybug flies, the elytra pop open. They give the first pair of wings room to flap and flutter. When the ladybug lands, the wings go down, and the elytra close shut over them.

The ladybug has three main body parts—the head, the thorax, and the abdomen. The head contains eyes, mouth parts, and antennae. The ladybug's mouth has pincers to chew its food. The thorax consists of three pairs of legs and the two pairs of wings. The abdomen contains organs that help the ladybug digest its food and reproduce.

Ladybug with
open elytra

Why Do Farmers Love Ladybugs?

The favorite food of ladybugs is tiny insects called aphids *(AY fihdz)*. Aphids feed on plant juices. When ladybugs eat aphids, they are doing farmers a big favor.

In the late 1800's, a pest called the cottony cushion scale insect was eating the citrus crop in California. The farmers brought in a species of ladybug from Australia. The ladybugs ate the scale insects and saved the crop. Since then, ladybugs have been one of our most important pest controls.

In the fall, ladybugs gather together in huge groups on the ground and hibernate until spring. Some people gather sleeping ladybugs in buckets and sell them to gardeners and farmers.

Ladybug eating aphids

15

How Did Ladybugs Get Their Name?

Not all ladybugs are "ladies." There are both male and female ladybugs. So how did they get their name? In the Middle Ages, farmers were grateful to the little beetles for saving their crops. They believed the way the ladybugs ate "bad" insects was a miracle that came from God. So the farmers named the insect after Mary, Jesus's mother, who is also known as "Our Lady."

In England, ladybugs are called ladybirds. Perhaps you've heard this nursery rhyme:

> Ladybird, Ladybird,
> Fly away home.
> Your house is on fire,
> And your children all gone.

The nursery rhyme started from the practice of farmers burning certain fields after harvest. They wanted the ladybugs to fly away so that they could be safe and return to eat more insects. And that's exactly what ladybugs have done for centuries!

Group of ladybugs

When Does a Ladybug Look Like a Lizard?

Ladybugs go through four stages before they become adults. First there are the eggs laid by an adult female. The eggs hatch in the spring or summer as larvae *(LAHR vee)*. Ladybug larvae are often brightly colored, and they look like tiny lizards.

The larvae eat all the time and use food energy to grow. After about three to six weeks, the larvae transform into pupae *(PYOO pee)*.

The pupae resemble adult ladybugs, but they have softer bodies and tiny, padlike wings. The pupae develop and finally shed their old bodies. Full-grown ladybugs emerge. Males and females mate, the females lay eggs, and the cycle starts all over again.

Ladybug larva

Is the Weevil Really Evil?

Yes, weevils are evil beetles—as far as gardeners and farmers are concerned. If the ladybug does good by eating other insects, the weevil does harm by eating plants.

Name almost any grain, fruit, or vegetable, and it is likely that at least one kind of weevil enjoys eating it. The boll weevil eats cotton. The granary weevil eats wheat and other seeds. The rice weevil goes after rice and other cereals. One kind of fruit weevil chomps on apples, cherries, and plums.

The weevil damages plants in two ways. First, it chews its way into the plants. Then it lays its eggs in the hole it has made. When the eggs hatch, the larvae eat through the plants from the inside out.

Boll weevil

Why Do Weevils Have Such Big Snouts?

A weevil's snout, or nose, is curved downward so that it can bore into plants. At the end of the long snout are the weevil's mouth parts that chew fruits, seeds, and other plant parts.

Different kinds of weevils have different kinds of snout shapes. Each shape is adapted to eating certain plants or parts of plants. For example, the female nut weevil's snout is often longer than its body. It needs a long snout to bore through the hard shell of a nut and to lay its eggs inside.

Weevil snout

23

Are Fireflies Flies, Bugs, or Beetles?

Fireflies are not really flies. Some people call them lightning bugs, but they are not bugs either. Fireflies are actually beetles.

The firefly is a flat, egg-shaped beetle 1/4 to 3/4 inches (5 to 20 millimeters) long. Its color is mostly brown or black. The firefly would be a rather ordinary beetle, except for one thing. At night, it can "light up." You probably have seen fireflies whizzing around and flashing their lights on warm summer nights.

Some firefly larvae can glow, too. This is why people call them glowworms. Of course, they are not worms at all.

Fireflies at night

How Do Fireflies Make That "Cool" Light?

The firefly's light is cool in more ways than one. Unlike natural and human-made light, it gives off no heat. The firefly's light is produced by a complicated set of chemical reactions that take place in its abdomen. This complex process is called bioluminescence *(BY oh LOO muh NEHS uhns).*

There are three layers to the organ that produces the firefly's light. The innermost layer acts as a reflector. The middle layer contains the light cells. The outermost layer is clear and can be seen through.

Fireflies can control the light they produce. They send out light in a pattern of flashes. Scientists believe that fireflies do this by regulating the amount of oxygen they take into their bodies. Oxygen is the fuel that helps create the light.

Firefly's abdomen

What Do All Those Flashes Mean?

The male firefly flashes its light for a very important purpose. It wants to find a mate. When it gets dark, the male firefly flies through the night. It flashes its light like a signal. Each kind of firefly has its own signal.

The female firefly has short wings and often can't fly. It perches itself on a bush or a rock and waits. When a male passes by with a signal the female recognizes, the female flashes back the same signal. The male lands and touches the female's antennae. This is how fireflies smell each other. If the female smells right to him, the two fireflies will mate. Later the female lays her eggs.

Male firefly

How Did Click Beetles Get Their Name?

A few click beetles can glow like fireflies. But all click beetles have a special talent of their own that earned them their name—their ability to click.

The click beetle has a long and slender body. If it falls on its back, it has a clever way of turning itself over. The click beetle locks two segments of its thorax together with a hooklike part. The two segments press together. When the beetle releases the hook, it makes a clicking noise and flips into the air. If it is lucky, the beetle lands on its feet. If not, it keeps on clicking until it does.

Sometimes the click beetle makes its clicking noise to scare off predators, animals such as birds or lizards that want to eat it.

Click beetle

What Is the Bombardier Beetle's Secret Weapon?

Many beetles have special ways of protecting themselves from predators. The bombardier *(bahm buh DIHR)* beetle produces two chemicals in separate parts of its body. When a predator attacks, the chemicals mix together in another body part. The chemical reaction causes a kind of explosion. The beetle squirts the burning mix of chemicals out of its abdomen and straight at the predator. The predator doesn't like this and quickly leaves.

Sometimes the predator may already have the bombardier beetle in its mouth when the beetle squirts out its secret weapon. Then the surprised predator spits out the beetle and runs off with a bad taste in its mouth.

Bombardier beetle

33

How Do Some Beetles Play Tricks?

Some beetles camouflage *(KAM uh flahzh),* or cover themselves up, so that predators cannot see them. Cryptic *(KRIHP tihk)* beetles have bodies that blend into tree bark, leaves, and other parts of their environment. The darkling beetle you see here is one kind of cryptic beetle.

Most jewel beetles have bright, shiny colors. For some, these colors help attract their prey. Other jewel beetles have colors that fool their predators. For example, some have spots of bright color on their elytra that look like eyes. When they display their elytra, the "eyes" look right at the predator and startle it. This gives the beetle time to fly away to safety.

Darkling beetle

When Is a Beetle Not Like a Beetle?

When it is trying to look like another insect, that's when! This is called mimicry *(MIM ihk ree)*. Mimicry is another weapon beetles use to keep predators away. They look and behave like other insects, such as ants, that predators know can fight back. Other beetles mimic flies and butterflies that are fast moving and hard to catch.

The wasp beetle has a long, tapered body that is yellow and black like a wasp's. Another type of beetle looks like a bumblebee and will try to "sting" any animal that captures it. That should be enough to scare off even the bravest predator!

Wasp beetle

Why Are Some Scarabs Called Tumblebugs?

Scarabs *(SKAR uhbz)* form another family of beetles that numbers 20,000 species. Scarabs have thick and shiny shells that reflect the sun. Japanese beetles and Junebugs are scarabs.

The tumblebug is a scarab that eats dung, the solid waste of animals. The tumblebug shapes the dung into a ball and rolls it until it is smooth and solid. Along the way, the beetle may tumble down numerous times, which is how it earned its name. Sometimes, as in the picture, two or more tumblebugs work together to roll the ball.

When the tumblebug finds a safe spot, it lays its egg into the ball and buries it in the ground. When the egg hatches, the larva eats the dung for food. Later, the scarab emerges from the earth as an adult.

Tumblebugs

39

Which Ancient People Worshiped Scarabs?

Thousands of years ago, the ancient Egyptians saw scarabs rolling their dung balls. They used this image as one of the symbols of the sun god, who rolled the sun across the sky each day. When the newborn scarabs emerged from the earth, the Egyptians saw them as a sign of immortality. The Egyptians may even have gotten the idea of making human mummies from the scarab pupa formed inside the dung ball.

Pictures of scarabs have been found on Egyptian scrolls, in works of art, and as decorative designs on the walls of tombs. Scarabs were carved out of precious stones and worn as rings or other jewelry. Carved scarabs were also placed in the tombs of the dead. Ancient Egyptians thought the carvings would bring the dead good fortune in the afterlife.

Scarab in Egyptian art

Does the Elephant Beetle Have a Trunk?

No, but it does have horns—five of them—that look like tusks! The elephant beetle is a member of the scarab family, and it is one of the largest beetles in the world. It uses its horns to defend its food source, which is the flowing sap from wounds in tree limbs.

The elephant beetle lives in the rain forests of Central and South America. The heat and moisture there help produce the largest beetles in the world. Other large-horned beetles from the tropics include the rhinoceros beetle, the Atlas beetle, and the Hercules beetle. These last two are named for a Greek god and a Greek hero, both known for their great strength.

Elephant beetle

43

What Is the World's Heaviest Insect?

The supersized Goliath beetle of Africa is the world's heaviest insect. This beetle can weigh as much as 3 1/2 ounces (99 grams) or more. This beetle is named for the giant in the Bible who was killed in battle by the shepherd boy David.

Like the giant Goliath, the Goliath beetle is big and awkward. When this beetle flies, it has a hard time staying airborne in rough weather. It twists and turns its legs while flying to keep its balance. This action is similar to the way a top spins to remain upright.

Goliath beetle

How Do Stag Beetles Use Their "Antlers"?

Stag beetles have horns like Goliath beetles, but they are set on either side of the head. The horns look like the antlers of a stag, a male deer. They are actually the beetle's mandibles *(MAN duh buhlz),* or jaws. The antlers of some beetles are almost as long as their bodies!

Stag beetles use their antlers to fight other males for females. The males lock horns to see which is the stronger beetle. The winner often tosses its rival into the air. Then the winner may carry off the female as its prize.

Only a few stag beetles can use their mandibles to pinch or bite. The others are harmless to humans.

Stag beetles

How Ferocious Is the Tiger Beetle?

Like the big cat it is named for, the tiger beetle is a ferocious predator that eats other insects. But the tiger beetle's larva is even more ferocious.

The wormlike larva lives in a burrow in the ground. It uses hooks to hang onto the wall of the burrow. Then it waits. When another insect comes close to the burrow, the larva attacks. It jumps out and sinks its jaws into its prey. Then it drags the helpless insect into its burrow and eats it.

Tiger beetle larva

How Do Desert Beetles Beat the Heat?

Desert beetles are well adapted to their hot, harsh environment. They are wingless and unable to fly. To get away from the hot sun, they dive deep into the sand. Below the surface there is more moisture. There are also cooler temperatures. When the sun sets, the desert cools down, and the desert beetles pop out of the sand. Then they begin their nightly hunt for food.

Some desert beetles have arched elytra. There is a space inside for air. This air pocket helps protect them from the heat.

This Namibian *(nuh MIHB ee uhn)* desert beetle of southern Africa has long, stiltlike legs. When the sand gets hot, the beetle rises up on its legs. This keeps its body as far away from the hot sand as possible.

Stilt-legged
desert beetle

How Do Diving Beetles Breathe Underwater?

Desert beetles dive into the sand to keep cool. Diving beetles dive into the water to hunt for snails, tadpoles, and small fish.

The diving beetle is one kind of water beetle that lives in ponds and streams. It has a long, oval body good for floating and diving. Its long legs move together like oars as it swims through the water.

A bubble of oxygen is trapped under its elytra or body hair when it dives. This allows the diving beetle to breathe underwater for a long time. The diving beetle sometimes hangs upside down in the water. This allows it to draw more oxygen into its body through openings between its elytra and abdomen.

Diving beetle

53

Why Do Whirligig Beetles Spin?

When the whirligig *(HWUR lee gihg)* beetle sees prey, it spins around quickly to catch it. The whirligig beetle is another kind of water beetle. Its dark, oval body is well equipped to float. Its paddle-shaped hind legs help it skim and spin across the water.

The whirligig beetle has compound eyes that are divided in two. The upper half of each of its eyes sees on or along the water. The lower half sees underwater and looks for small fish and insect larvae to eat.

On a pond, you might see as many as a hundred whirligigs spinning around in zigzag patterns. But never once will one whirligig bump into another. A special organ in its antennae "picks up" echoes of sound waves bouncing off objects in the water. This helps the whirligig avoid collisions!

Whirligig beetles

Why Do Some People Think Beetles Are the Greatest?

People have found many uses for beetles. Ladybugs and other beetles are important pest controls for plant-eating insects. Jewel beetles and weevils get rid of fast-growing weeds. The beetles lay eggs on the weeds, and their larvae eat away at it.

Beetle shapes and designs are used in the jewelry that is popular in many parts of the world. The bodies and elytra of dead beetles have themselves been made into jewelry. In Mexico, live beetles are decorated with glass beads, fastened to small chains, and actually pinned to a person's clothing!

Some people, however, would rather eat beetles than wear them. In parts of Asia, Africa, and Australia, beetles and beetle larvae are favorite foods.

Cooked beetle larvae

57

How Are Beetles Good Environmentalists?

Beetles do far more to protect the environment than most people imagine. They are excellent recyclers. Beetles bury dead animals and plant material. By doing this, beetles help enrich the soil.

Tumblebugs and other dung beetles remove animal dung from the earth's surface. This increases pastureland and prevents disease from spreading from flies and other insects that lay eggs in the dung.

Beetle and larvae
with carcass

59

Are Beetles in Danger?

Some are! As land becomes developed, some beetles are losing the forests and waterways they live in. Predators such as rats and birds eat other beetles into extinction. In turn, the beetles that live on the dead bodies of certain animals have no food to eat when these animals disappear from their habitat.

The Endangered Species Act (ESA) of 1973 was set up to protect all endangered animals, including beetles. Twelve species of beetles are protected by the ESA in the United States, including the northeastern beach tiger beetle seen here. Any person who harms one of these beetles or its habitat can be fined or arrested.

But this kind of protection is often not enough. Some endangered beetles are raised in laboratories. Later, they may be released back into the wild.

Northeastern beach
tiger beetle

Beetle Fun Facts

→ Many kinds of beetles have strange names. For example, there is the wrinkled bark beetle, the long-toed water beetle, the pleasing fungus beetle, and the deathwatch beetle.

→ Beetles vary greatly in the number of eggs the female produces at one time. A dung beetle may lay only 5 to 7 eggs, while the blister beetle may lay 2,000 to 10,000 eggs at once.

→ Carpet beetles are the goats of the beetle world in that they can eat almost anything. These insects can feed on and digest hoofs, hair, claws, feathers, and wool. The digestive juices in their stomachs are capable of breaking down almost anything.

→ The tortoise beetle of Central America can change its color in 20 minutes—just as a chameleon can.

→ Beetle blood may be yellow, green, or orange.

→ A few kinds of click beetles glow like fireflies. In Brazil, night travelers sometimes tie a pair of these glowing beetles to their big toes to light the path ahead.

→ It takes 80,000 fireflies to produce the same amount of light produced by one candle.

→ The giant stag beetle remains in the larvae stage for five to eight years.

Glossary

abdomen The third part of an insect's body.

adapted Changed to be good for doing something.

antennae The pair of feelers on an insect's head.

chemical reaction Something that happens when chemicals come together.

compound eye An eye with many parts

cycle Changes that always happen one after another at special times.

develop To start and grow.

emerge To come out and be seen.

environment Things all around an animal or a person.

endangered In danger of dying out.

extinction The act of doing away with, or killing off, completely.

habitat An animal's home.

insect A small animal without a backbone, with three body parts, three pairs of legs, and two pairs of wings.

larva A newly hatched baby insect.

moisture Water in the air or the earth.

organ A big body part that does a special job.

oxygen A gas in the air needed for breathing.

pincer A large claw.

prey Animals that other animals eat.

pupa A baby insect between larva and winged adult.

predator An animal eater.

signal Something, such as a light, that has a special meaning.

species A group of the same kind of animals.

stage A time of growing.

thorax The second part of an insect's body, between the head and abdomen.

transform To change shape.

Index

(**Boldface** indicates a photo, map, or illustration.)

For more information about beetles, try these resources:

Beetles, by Kathleen Derzipilski, Marshall Cavendish Corp., 2004

Beetles, by Peter Murray, Child's World, 2002

Beetles: The Most Common Insect, by Sara Swan Miller, Franklin Watts, 2001

http://members.aol.com/YESedu/home.html

http://tolweb.org/tree?group=Coleoptera&contgroup=Endopterygota

http://www.nysaes.cornell.edu/ent/biocontrol/predators/ladybintro.html

Beetle Classification

Scientists classify animals by placing them into groups. The animal kingdom is a group that contains all the world's animals. Phylum, class, order, and family are smaller groups. Each phylum contains many classes. A class contains orders, an order contains families, and a family contains individual species. Each species also has its own scientific name. Here is how the animals in this book fit in to this system.

Insects and their relatives (Phylum Arthropoda)

Insects (Class Insecta)

Beetles (Order Coleoptera)

Carpet beetles and their relatives (Family Dermestidae)

Darkling beetles and stilt-legged desert beetles (Family Tenebrionidae)

Deathwatch beetles (Family Anobiidae)

Diving beetles (Family Dytiscidae)

Feather-winged beetles (Family Ptiliidae)

Fireflies (Family Lampyridae)

Bombadier beetles and their relatives (Family Carabidae)

Jewel beetles (Family Buprestidae)

Junebugs, tumblebugs, and other scarab beetles (Family Scarabaeidae)
African goliath beetle.............................. *Goliathus goliatus*
Atlas beetle .... *Chalcosoma caucasus*
Elephant beetle .... *Megasoma elaphus*
Hercules beetle .... *Dynastes hercules*
Japanese beetle................................. *Popillia japonica*
Rhinoceros beetle .... *Oryctes rhinoceros*

Ladybugs (Family Coccinellidae)

Wasp beetle and its relatives (Family Cerambycidae)
Wasp beetle.................................... *Clytus arietis*

Long-toed water beetles (Family Dryopidae)

Pleasing fungus beetles (Family Erotylidae)

Stag beetles (Family Lucanidae)
Giant stag beetle .... *Lucanus elaphus*

Tiger beetles (Family Cicindelidae)
Northeastern beach tiger beetle .... *Cicindela dorsalis dorsalis*

Tortoise beetles and their relatives (Family Chrysomelidae)

Weevils and their relatives (Family Curculionidae)
Boll weevil..................................... *Anthonomus grandis*
Granary weevil .... *Sitophilus granarius*
Rice weevil .... *Sitophilus oryzae*

Whirligig beetles (Family Gyrinidae)

Wrinkled bark beetles (Family Rhysodidae)